ee you."

"You did it!" a temple

of the

Holy Spirit."

ou. You brighten my life."

"I'll never forget your birthday.

Words

The day you were born

was one of the most

important days of my life."

ave a surprise for you."

PRESENTED TO

FROM

DATE

LOVING WORDS

Every Child Needs to Hear

Encouragment and Comfort for a Child's Heart

ED ANDERSON
AND
JOHN E. PETERSON

COUNTRYMAN

A J. Countryman book.

Editorial development and design production by
Koechel Peterson & Associates, Minneapolis, MN.

"A Prayer for the World's Children"© Ina Hughs, excerpted from *A Prayer for Children*
published by William Morrow & Company. Used by permission.

Photography by Tom Henry

ISBN: 08499-5404-5

Printed and bound in Belgium

INTRODUCTION

---

*Children are the world's greatest imitators. And parents
have no greater joy than hearing the first words their baby has to say.
All the more important, then, that the first words a child hears be loving
words. Behavioral scientists tell us that even from the womb babies can recognize
voices, and children of all ages sense the power of loving words to calm, to
heal, to teach, and encourage. That is because words have the power to create
or to destroy. With loving words and a loving heart you can help your child
grow into a confident, happy adult who feels worthy of all the blessings
life has to offer and who will one day return the love received.*

*Loving words from a parent, a grandparent, or guardian can lay
the foundation for a positive, healthy self-image and empower a child to view
the world as a place where every dream can become a possible reality. There
is no greater gift a parent can give a child. Nor is there anything more
empowering than a positive belief in yourself and God who created you.*

*As a child you needed to hear loving words. As an adult you will love to
say them. What better way for a child to start out right in life.*

"Death and life are in the power of the tongue."
Proverbs 18:21

"I have a surprise for you."

WORDS THAT SHOW
Love

"Our home
would be
very empty
without you."

"It's fun to be with

"You give the best hugs."

*"But now, O LORD,
You are our Father; we
are the clay, and You our potter;
and all we are the work of Your hand."
Isaiah 64:8*

"One of my best memories is of you curled up on my lap while I read to you. You were so cozy."

"A candle loses nothing by lighting another candle."
Unknown

"I'll never forget your birthday. The day you were born you. You brighten my life." was one of the most important days of my life."

"I love you just the way you are. You don't have to be like anybody else."

"Welcome home
to your new family ...

*we've been
waiting for you."*

This new life is ready for your loving words, your

loving instructions, and your loving ways. This little

one has been hand-picked for your home, your arms,

and your heart. How you raise this baby matters.

"There's nobody else in the
I'm glad you're mine."

Wouldn't it be wonderful if all children could

grow up being reaffirmed for all the wonderful little

things they do. Just because they're who they are.

Think what the world would be like.

whole world quite like you.

"Someday,

because I love you

when you're a mommy,
you'll understand
that sometimes I say 'no'
only because
I love you."

Children need a positive

example they can follow

in the family, namely,

their parents.

No amount of love is too much for any child.

A parent who loves his child gives the best

gift of all—the gift of himself.

"You give the best

hugs.

"A child's spirit is like a child. You can never catch it by running after it; you must stand still, and for love it will soon itself come back."
Arthur Miller

"Your smile is so contagious,

Celebrate the little "rites of

passage" when they happen . . .

and remember you only pass this

way once. . . . Don't miss it.

I can't help

"Rejoice with those who rejoice."

Romans 12:15

but smile back at you."

Humor is a great companion. Kids love

to be silly. They enjoy the unexpected and

the absurd. They look for surprises and love

to laugh. Get down on their level. Speak

at their level. And listen at their level.

"I can't believe we lost

"A merry heart does good, like medicine."

Proverbs 17:22

that baseball you hit.
It must still be in the air."

"I love you just the way you are.
You don't have to be like anybody else."

WORDS THAT SHOW *Respect*

"I love you,

but that doesn't mean

I like everything you do."

"Your dreams for the future

"Your failures won't hurt you
unless you start blaming
them on others."

Unknown

"I will always stand by you,

no matter what."

"*Your anger won't push me away.*

I still love you."

Say "YES!" as often as you can.

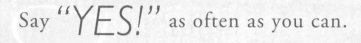

matter to me."

"*It's good to see you.*"

"You two did such

a great job shoveling the walk."

words of praise

All too often there is a parental formula used of

heavy on criticism and light on praise that causes

children to go through life feeling inadequate

and unworthy of love. An easy way to circumvent

this is to intentionally let your children overhear

the nice things you say about them to others.

"I'd like

The key to connecting with a child is to listen.

Children love to be listened to.

to know what's on your mind."

Your open mind and your open heart

will make it easier for your child to tell you

what is on his mind.

Loving In Disguise

"Be careful!"
Translation (what you are really thinking):
"It breaks my heart to see you hurt."

"I don't like that kind of behavior."
Translation: *"It could hurt you."*

While disciplining a child you say,
"This hurts me more than it hurts you."
Translation: *"I can't stand this; I want to get this over as soon
as possible and forget it ever happened."*

"You're like your father."
Translation: *"You look like a man to me."*

"What do you mean you didn't get all A's?"
Translation: *"I think you're a genius no matter what your teachers say."*

"Let your speech always be with grace."

Colossians 4:6

"Don't forget to wear your boots today."
Translation: *"I love you so much, I don't want you to be uncomfortable."*

"Eat your peas and carrots."
Translation: *"I want you to be strong and healthy."*

"I can't believe you did that."
Translation: *"I live in a fantasy world when it comes to you."*

"I can't understand how your friends could be so mean to you."
Translation: *"I can't stand for anything hateful or evil to touch you."*

"Your mother and I . . . (fill in the blank).
Translation: *"This is heavy-duty stuff; it's why we've already discussed it before talking with you."*

"Your room is such a mess."
Translation: *"I want you to be the perfect child."*

As your children pass from childhood

to adolescence they need to be reminded

of your love and concern. Take time to

notice. And enjoy those moments together.

woman you're becoming."

you

"Let no one seek his own,

but each one the other's well-being."

1 Corinthians 10:24

"When children are

little they make our

heads ache; when

grown, our hearts."

Italian Proverb

"Your dreams

One thing you can give your children that

is priceless is a heritage of love and positive

reinforcement. Let them know you're there

to help them—no matter what!

"Here is a book I really enjoyed reading."

WORDS THAT
Teach

"You are
a temple
of the
Holy Spirit."

"How would you

"Could I show you how to do that?"

*"They found Him in the temple, sitting
in the midst of the teachers, both listening
to them and asking them questions."*
Luke 2:46

"Would you like to know what I think about that?"

"I remember when

I used to sit and

watch your grandpa

painting our old fence, too."

like to go to work with me?"

"Do you need help

with any of your

homework?"

Affirmation

Praise the acts of kindness and

generosity of your children.

Doing so is a positive reinforcement

of their spiritual development.

"That is one of the nicest things

I've ever seen you do."

"*Bear one another's burdens.*"

Galatians 6:2

Can you imagine a more positive statement

you could ever make to any child?

Especially when you see him going out of

his way to help someone less fortunate.

"You're a blessing sent from God."

When you see your children sowing seeds

of kindness, don't let the moment go by

unnoticed. Celebrate it.

Learning to parent your child by emphatically

understanding the world of your child as your child

"Help me see what you

perceives it is a bonding experience.

"For I know the thoughts that I think toward

you, says the LORD, thoughts of peace and not

of evil, to give you a future and a hope."

Jeremiah 29:11

see."

"The tough

Be aware your child is watching you. He dreams

of getting "big." Doing what men do. Living like

he's got the world in his hands. He really does, and

you're going to hand it to him.

part is gonna be taking the lather
off with a razor
but leaving the skin . . .
so, watch carefully now."

"You rascal,
        I taught your dad that move.

"Grandchildren
are God's way of
compensating us
for growing old."

Mary H. Waldrip

I bet he'd love to see you
                beat your grandpa.

Playing together spans generations. Be sure to include it in your to-do list. There will be at least one grateful child.

"Children's children are the crown of old men."

Proverbs 17:6

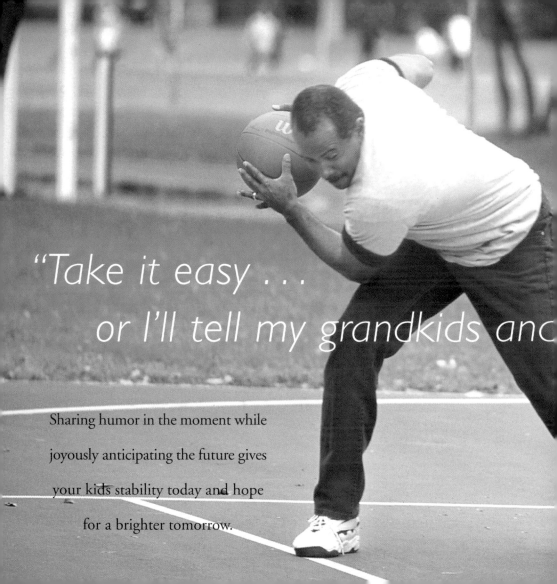

"Take it easy ...
    or I'll tell my grandkids and

Sharing humor in the moment while

joyously anticipating the future gives

your kids stability today and hope

for a brighter tomorrow.

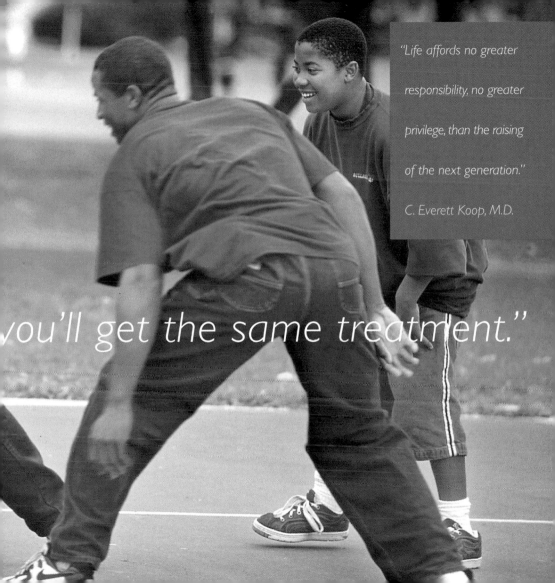

"Life affords no greater responsibility, no greater privilege, than the raising of the next generation."

C. Everett Koop, M.D.

you'll get the same treatment."

Spend

speaking without

Speaking Without Words
50 Things to Do Together

Find the first flower of spring.

Write a letter to a grandparent or elderly person who lives alone.

See how long it takes to drive a bucket of balls
at the driving range. How far did you drive them?

Watch videos of TV shows popular
with children during the '50s and '60s.

Work on a photo album together.

Make a funny video together.

Establish the tradition of celebrating an unusual
or little known holiday together, such as Hanukkah.

Read everything Jesus said in the Bible.

the day at the beach together.

Bake and decorate a cake for no reason at all.

Go out for breakfast together once a month.

Go on a bike ride together

Wear your clothes backwards to a meal and see if anyone notices what you two have done.

Capture lightning bugs in a jar (to be released unharmed).

In the fall, take a trip together to see colorful leaves.

Design and create your own gift-wrap for your exclusive use.

Eat a meal together using only pig-Latin to communicate.

Interview each other to obtain your life stories and record them on audio or videotape.

Build a birdhouse.

Write letters or notes to each other using a feather or reed you have cut to a point.

Work out and run a long-distance race together.

Pick apples and make a pie together.

Help your child find your town on a map.

Take a nature hike together.

In the winter, make snow people together.
Use your family as models.

Ride a city bus downtown to Christmas shop.

Volunteer to serve food at a homeless shelter. If it is permitted,
talk to the homeless when you have completed your task.

Share the details of your child's birth day.

Make finger puppets with your child. Cut the ends
off the fingers of old gloves. Draw faces on the fingers
with felt tip markers and glue on yarn for hair.

Become "Secret Santas" to needy kids.
Dress up in Santa outfits while wrapping the gifts.

Bake Christmas cookies together.

Go Christmas caroling together.

Cut a snack, such as an apple or orange, into equal
parts and talk about fractions with your child.

Go to the park together.

Have your child be a pet detective and observe an animal. Report the findings in a "log."

Make a time capsule with your child and save it for a year or two. Place objects of current interest in a coffee can and bury it. Mark the spot.

Take golf or tennis lessons together.

Go go-carting together.

Go horseback riding together.

Invite a person who lives alone to a dinner you prepared together.

Practice a music instrument together.

Be silly. Show up at the dinner table with Groucho Marx nose and glasses to discuss an uncomfortable subject.

"Behold, children are a heritage from the LORD,

the fruit of the womb is a reward....

Happy is the man who has his quiver full of them."

Psalm 127:3, 5

Memorize the books of the Bible.

Memorize the presidents of the U.S.

Write a thank-you note to the child's teacher at the end of the school year.

Take up the same hobby (photography, collecting, woodworking, etc.)

Write a short story together.

Go fishing together.

Read the same book and then discuss it.

"I know you can do it. Keep trying."

WORDS THAT *Empower*

"You did it!"

"You've worked hard.

"Let no one despise your youth,
but be an example to the believers
in word, in conduct, in love, in spirit,
in faith, in purity."

1 Timothy 4:12

"The cards you make yourself are my very favorite! Thank you."

"Great game— let's go celebrate!"

You can be proud of yourself."

I'm proud of you.

"You are trying so hard; the rest of my weekend is yours."

"Encouragement is oxygen for the soul."
Unknown

"So you thought

Someday your child will outrun you, but

until then she needs you to keep up a steady

pace of encouragement and nourishment.

Your role is key to her maturity.

you could outrun your dad."

"Good game; let's celebrate!"

"What's done to children, they will do to society."

Dr. Karl Menninger

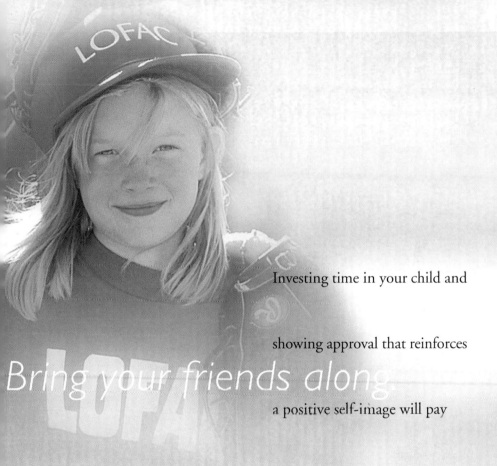

Bring your friends along

Investing time in your child and

showing approval that reinforces

a positive self-image will pay

dividends for years to come.

"I was lucky today that you

the power

of affirmation

"Your hands have made me and fashioned
me.... You have granted me life and favor,
and Your care has preserved my spirit."
Job 10:8, 12

weren't twenty years older."

"What

"Whatever your hand finds to do,

do it with your might."

Ecclesiastes 9:10

a great imagination you have."

Locked inside every child is a creative place.

That place is filled to the very top with potential.

In that spot you'll find enormous possibilities.

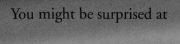

You might be surprised at

what your child creates.

He could be an Einstein,

a Picasso, Gates, or

Spielberg. You'll only

know if you encourage

those creative efforts.

"Turn around and let

"Jesus said, 'Let the little children come to Me, and do not forbid them; for of such is the kingdom of heaven.' And He laid His hands on them."

Matthew 19:14, 15

"Every child is an artist. The problem is how to remain an artist once he grows up."

Pablo Picasso

Dad see this."

"Whatever you do,

do it heartily."

Colossians 3:23

"All your practicing has paid off.

Let your children hear your words of approval.

Take pride in their accomplishments.

State your feelings as if they were the

most important feelings in the world.

I can hardly believe what I hear!"

One of the best ways to have

a lasting relationship with

your children is to create

lasting memories with them.

"Let's go have

fun together."

Our role as parents is to offer guidance

and to give our children opportunities

to make more informed decisions.

" I pray for you

A child who seeks and finds what

God has planned for her will have a

more productive career and greater

success in finding a compatible mate.

"Train up a child in

the way he should go."

Proverbs 22:6

every day."

"The way I talked to you was wrong.
Will you forgive me?"

WORDS THAT *Heal*

"Your fears

are not

silly."

"No excuses. I'm sorry!

"Whoever causes one of these little ones who believe
in Me to sin, it would be better for him if a
millstone were hung around his neck, and he
were drowned in the depth of the sea."
Matthew 18:6

> "I shall allow no man
> to belittle my soul
> by making me hate him."
>
> *Booker T. Washington*

"There are times when we all
need to be alone.
Take some time for yourself."

"Grandma and Grandpa

can tell you that

I was disobedient sometimes

and that I got in trouble

with them."

I forgive you

Please forgive me."

"OOPS!"

"I should not have lost my temper. I'm sorry!"

Always be aware

that there is a brief

magical moment

in every relationship

when the right

statement will

change a life forever.

"It's okay. I know you

"The child has a primary need from the very beginning of her life to be regarded and respected as the person she really is at any given time."

Alice Miller

didn't mean to break it."

There are times when encouragement means a lot,

and a word is enough to convey it.

At such times—Listen! With your *ears, your mind, and your heart*. Listen for the meaning behind your child's action. Listen for the message behind the words.

"Before you tell me about it . . .

"What a mother says to her children is not heard by the world; but it will be heard by posterity."

Jean Paul Richter

"Confess your trespasses to one another, and pray for
one another, that you may be healed."

James 5:16

remember I was
your age once, too."

"I know it was embarrassing, but thank you"

Sooner or later every child is confronted with a choice—telling a lie to cover something up or telling the truth and being corrected. How we handle these moments as parents will determine to a great extent the truthfulness of our children.

"If a child tells a lie, tell him (her) that he has told a lie, but don't call him a liar. If you define him as a liar, you'll break down his confidence in his own character."
JOHANN PAUL FRIEDRICH

for telling the truth."

The point made is that by restricting criticism to a specific bad act, a parent is unlikely to damage a child's self-image. Likewise, to praise a child for truthfulness reinforces a positive self-image.

"Don't worry about it, honey.

As long as you're

"He who restrains his lips is wise."

Proverbs 10:19

Loving words that communicate

empathy and support can teach children

invaluable lessons while reaffirming a

parent's unwavering love.

okay, *that's all that matters.*"

A Prayer for the World's Children

(To be shared with your children)

We pray for children

who sneak popsicles before supper,

who erase holes in math workbooks,

who can never find their shoes.

And we pray for those

who stare at photographers from behind barbed wire,

who can't bound down the street in a new pair of sneakers,

who never "counted potatoes,"

who are born in places we wouldn't be caught dead,

who never go to the circus,

who live in an X-rated world.

We pray for children

who bring us sticky kisses and fistfulls of dandelions,

who hug us in a hurry and forget their lunch money.

And we pray for those

who never get dessert,

who have no safe blanket to drag behind them,

who watch their parents watch them die,

who can't find any bread to steal,

who don't have any rooms to clean up,

whose pictures aren't on anybody's dresser,

whose monsters are real.

We pray for children

who spend all their allowances before Tuesday,

who throw tantrums in the grocery store

    and pick at their food,

who like ghost stories,

who shove dirty clothes under the bed

    and never rinse out the tub,

who get visits from the tooth fairy,

who don't like to be kissed in front of the carpool,

who squirm in church or temple and scream in the phone,

whose tears we sometimes laugh at and whose

    smiles can make us cry.

And we pray for those

whose nightmares come in the daytime,

who will eat anything,

who have never seen a dentist,

who aren't spoiled by anyone,

who go to bed hungry and cry themselves to sleep,

who live and move, but have no being.

We pray for children who want to
be carried and for those who must,

for those who never give up and for those who don't get a

second chance, for those we smother…and for those who

will grab the hand of anyone kind enough to offer it.

Amen.

Ina Hughs

"I was wrong to raise my voice at you. I'm sorry."

Henry Wadsworth Longfellow once wrote,

"A torn jacket is soon mended, but hard words

bruise the heart of a child."

And just as "hard words bruise the heart of a child,"

so too can loving words *heal* the heart of a child.

RESOURCES

Try a new vacation spot, or new CD, or new book with your children. These are some resources.

VACATIONS

Educated Traveler
You and your children learn as you vacation.
1-800-648-5168

Walt Disney World and Disneyland
1-888-359-2255

Family Cruises
Familycruises.com

Rascals in Paradise
U.S.A., Canada, Europe, Africa, and Asia— specializes in vacations with children.
1-800-U-RASCAL

Surf and Sun Vacations
1-888-813-9320

Consider seeing:
Mount Rushmore, the Black Hills, and Badlands in western South Dakota
Washington, DC
Williamsburg, PA
A famous zoo or amusement park

Consider doing:
Rafting
Working on a ranch
Skiing
Biking

B O O K S

A Bear Called Paddington by Michael Bond
Winnie-the-Pooh by A. A. Milne
Oh, the Places You'll Go! or anything by Dr. Seuss
Anne of Green Gables by Lucy Maud Montgomery
A Wrinkle in Time by Madeleine L'Engle
The Crippled Lamb by Max Lucado
The Relatives Came by Cynthia Rylant
Paw Paw Chuck by Charles Swindoll
Alexander, Who Used to Be Rich Last Sunday by Judith Viorst
Alexander and the Terrible, Horrible, No Good, Very Bad Day by Judith Viorst
The Velveteen Rabbit by Margery Williams
The Narnia Chronicles series by C. S. Lewis
The Bible

B O O K S F O R P A R E N T S

The Only Kids Party Book You'll Ever Need by Gill Dickenson and Julia Goodwin
The New Parent: The Essential Guide by Dr. Miriam Stoppard
Becoming the Parent God Wants You to Be by Kevin Leman

M U S I C

Adventures in Odyssey audio and video series
RPM Righteous Pop Music, Vols. I and II, available from One Way Street, Inc., P.O. Box 5077, Englewood, CO 80155
G.T. and the Halo Express, an audio series
The Donut Man series

A WORD FROM THE PUBLISHER

Everyone remembers a person in their life who was there when desperately needed, a person who made a difference. Looking back at that moment we recall the details of that experience without really trying. We can hardly imagine living our life without that experience. We've all needed someone to love us, believe in us, be a role model for us, and challenge us. If you were fortunate to have all of that, you are a very lucky person. But some haven't.

There are a great many children without healthy role models who are desperately needing someone to make a difference in their lives. You can be that person. Why not take it on yourself to use Loving Words and be their role model? Read Loving Words, live Loving Words, and share Loving Words. Guaranteed, you will be someone's hero. And in the process, you will be surprised to learn that you have made a positive difference in your own life.

Always hoping and praying for God's Very Best for you and yours.

Jack Countryman